Making it a Success

of related interest

Asperger's Syndrome
A Guide for Parents and Professionals
Tony Attwood
ISBN 1 85302 577 1

Asperger Syndrome – What Teachers Need to Know
Matt Winter
Written for Cloud 9 Children's Foundation
ISBN 1 84310 143 2

Specialist Support Approaches to Autism Spectrum Disorder
Students in Mainstream Settings
Sally Hewitt
ISBN 1 84310 290 0

The Little Class with the Big Personality
Experiences of Teaching a Class of Young Children with Autism
Fran Hunnisett
ISBN 1 84310 308 7

Nonverbal Learning Disabilities at School
Educating Students with NLD, Asperger Syndrome and Related Conditions
Pamela B. Tanguay
ISBN 1 85302 941 6

Incorporating Social Goals in the Classroom
A Guide for Teachers and Parents of Children with High-Functioning Autism
and Asperger Syndrome
Rebecca A. Moyes
ISBN 1 85302 967 X

Addressing the Challenging Behavior of Children with High-Functioning
Autism/Asperger Syndrome in the Classroom
A Guide for Teachers and Parents
Rebecca A. Moyes
ISBN 1 84310 719 8

My Social Stories Book
Edited by Carol Gray and Abbie L. White
Illustrated by Sean McAndrew
ISBN 1 85302 950 5

Making it a Success

Practical Strategies and Worksheets for Teaching Students with Autism Spectrum Disorder

Sue Larkey

Foreword by Tony Attwood

Jessica Kingsley Publishers
London and Philadelphia

Social Stories (pp. 48–49) from *Annette Joosten's Book of Cool Strategies: A Personal Social Script Workbook for Australian Primary-age Students* by A. Joosten (2003) Brisbane: Book in Hand. Reproduced with permission from the author.
Recipes (pp. 42–44) adapted from *Look, Cook and Learn*, with permission from the Western Autistic School, Victoria, Australia.
Illustrations on pp. 20, 36, 38, 39, 61, 65, 67, 81 and 82 are by Paul Nash.
Illustrations on pp. 13, 19, 20, 22, 40, 89 and 94–96 are by Val Brooks.
Illustrations on pp. 42–44 are by Chioma Ovuworie.

First published in 2005
by Jessica Kingsley Publishers
116 Pentonville Road
London N1 9JB, UK
and
400 Market Street, Suite 400
Philadelphia, PA 19106, USA

www.jkp.com

Copyright © Sue Larkey 2005
Foreword copyright © Tony Attwood 2005

Library of Congress Cataloging in Publication Data

Larkey, Sue, 1968-
    Making it a success : practical strategies and worksheets for teaching students with autism spectrum disorder / Sue Larkey ; foreword by Tony Attwood.
        p. cm.
    Includes bibliographical references and index.
    ISBN-10: 1-84310-204-8 (pbk.)
    ISBN-13: 978-1-84310-204-5 (pbk.)
    1. Autistic children—Education. 2. Autism. I. Title.
    LC4717.L37 2005
    371.94—dc22

573699

                                                    2004029583

British Library Cataloguing in Publication Data

A CIP catalogue record for this book is available from the British Library

ISBN-13: 978 1 84310 204 5

ISBN-10: 1 84310 204 8

Printed and Bound in Great Britain by
Athenaeum Press, Gateshead, Tyne and Wear

Contents

Foreword

The inclusion of a child with autism in a regular class can be a daunting experience for the child, as well as his or her teacher and the other children in the class. Unfortunately, teachers do not have the time to read academic textbooks and journals to determine why a child with autism is confused or unable to achieve a particular academic objective. They need easy and immediate access to advice and resources written in their own "language" by someone who understands children and the dynamics of a typical classroom.

Sue Larkey knows the problems associated with inclusion not only from her experience as a teacher herself, but also from her academic knowledge and qualifications and from her intuitive understanding of autism. She has a remarkable ability to identify and briefly explain the difficulties experienced by a child with autism in a regular classroom and to suggest realistic and practical strategies to improve abilities and behaviour. Her advice is succinct and wise. This book is precisely what teachers ask for and need.

The worksheets and activities can be photocopied, personalised and enjoyed by both the child with autism and other children in the class. Some of the ideas are based on conventional and proven strategies, while some suggestions are original and are destined to become part of the regular programmes for children with autism. The author does not want a teacher to just survive the inclusion of the child with autism in his or her class from day to day but to make the inclusion a success. Reading and applying the activities in Sue Larkey's new book will enable inclusion to be a success for everyone.

Tony Attwood

Introduction

This book is a practical guide for educators who encounter the challenge of having a student with autism spectrum disorder in their classroom and for families dealing with the everyday requirements of their child at home.

Autism spectrum disorder, which encompasses autism or Asperger's syndrome, is uniquely individual, with a wide variation in behaviours. This book provides over 500 successful and practical ideas allowing the professional or parent to select and implement the appropriate strategies for the individual student.

There are many textbooks and websites available which explain autism spectrum disorder in an academic way (see Useful Resources on p.117). This text provides a basic explanation of the characteristics of autism, suggests easy strategies and provides worksheets for the busy teacher to copy. The worksheets and strategies can be used as they are or made simpler or more complex to meet the individual student's needs. Parents will also find these activities of enormous help in the day to day life of their child at home.

Indeed this book will be extremely useful to professionals who may have a child with obsessive compulsive disorder, attention deficit hyperactive disorder or pervasive developmental disorder not otherwise specified (PDD-NOS) in their class or a student with no diagnosis but displaying some autistic characteristics.

Chapter 1

Successful Strategies for Work Tasks

The nature of autism spectrum disorder is such that at work times the students often:

- are not rewarded by the social interaction surrounding work time and need expectations spelled out very clearly

- demonstrate poor organizational skills

- have no way of predicting how long an activity will last

- are unsure where to start and when to finish an activity, and will often repeat an activity because they are unaware it has ended (hence many autistic repetitive behaviours, e.g. spinning)

- have no way of knowing or anticipating the order in which demands will be made

- have no anticipation of when they will get to do what they want to do

- are uncomfortable with all this uncertainty and unable to give their best concentration to the work itself.

Strategies

1. Workload

- It is very important that the student is given an achievable workload and has some control over the work. For example, give the student some choice. This may mean he can order the tasks or choose the reward when he completes the work (see "Feedback and rewards" on p.13).

- Have a definite end to the work (e.g. reinforcement, special activity, playtime etc.).

- A "schedule" is an effective tool for ordering work tasks (see "Schedules" on p.17), or you can have "start" and "finish" boxes or piles so the student can see how many worksheets he needs to do and how many he has completed.

- Use an analogue clock and put a red dot to indicate when the session will finish (e.g. when the big hand gets to the five). Please note that timers with a sound (buzz or ring) are often ineffective as the noise upsets the student.

2. Work tasks

- Ensure there is one familiar aspect to the task and tap into an area of interest or strength in order to reduce stress (e.g. counting activity if this is a strength).

- Present the same concept in many different ways. Long term exposure to the same task can create rigidity, boredom and difficulty with generalization.

- Use the student's interests and fixations to introduce a new or difficult task. This creates a calming effect in a demanding situation (e.g. a picture of his favourite Thomas the Tank Engine character on the corner of a worksheet!).

- Have a balance of high, medium and low levels of interests within the work tasks.

- Make tasks functional and relevant wherever possible. Students will resist tasks that have minimal meaning or relevance to them or have an unclear start and finish point.

- Have a clear start and finish point. On a writing or drawing task put a cross (X) on the page showing where to start, and a dot showing where to finish.

- Repeat tasks. The nature of autism spectrum disorder is such that the students enjoy repetitive tasks. Allow the student to complete the task a number of times. For example, the worksheets that are in this book can be reused many times. This enables the student to be successful.

3. Work environment

- Allocate a specific area for specific tasks.

- Use visual schedules (see "Schedules" on p.17).

- Ensure the student can predict what will happen next in the sequence.

- Ensure the student can understand what is required of him.

If you can set up a work area as illustrated below you will probably find the student is less distracted and able to complete tasks independently and successfully. If you have limited assistance with the student, use the time to set up work tasks so the student is set up for independent learning.

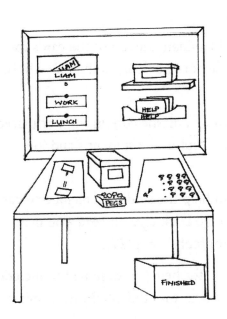 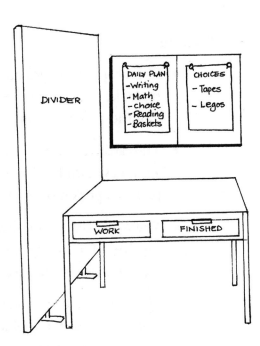

Figure 1 Work areas

4. Feedback and rewards

- Verbal information can be abstract or open to misinterpretation.

- Use statements of what you want, not what you don't want (e.g. "Draw a circle," rather than "Not a square," as the student might only hear "square").

- Demonstrate rather than explain. Remember to use visuals whenever possible.

- Trial rewards to ensure they are motivating.

- Compile a list of rewards with the student's family. You may be surprised by what motivates the student.

- Most rewards are functional, concrete and capable of immediate sensory feedback.

- Change the rewards frequently (you can repeat them later).

CARDS

The cards are designed to be used by both the teacher and the student. Many students forget what they wanted to ask the teacher, as there are so many distractions before their turn. If you can get the student to locate the relevant card before he leaves his desk or raises his hand, it will be more effective.

Instructions

- Photocopy the pages onto card and laminate them. For the cards for students, perhaps use the student's favourite colour, as then he will be motivated to use them.

- The cards can either be attached, using a plastic curtain ring, or placed in a business card holder, which can be kept in the student's and/or teacher's pocket or on their desk.

- You may need to add illustrations to help the student remember what the card says. For example, with "Please go back to your seat" you may include a picture of a seat (see "Pictographs" on p.27).

- The card "Have you asked _____ for help?" is designed to include the name of a buddy or volunteer rather than the student always coming straight to the teacher.

CARDS FOR STUDENTS

I need help	**I need a break for 5 minutes**
I don't know what to do	**Where do I start?**
Can you please help me?	**Where do I leave my work?**
How much time until I have finished?	**What do I do when I have finished?**
Can you tell me the instructions?	**I can't find my** _____
Toilet	**Wash hands**

CARDS FOR TEACHERS

Please wait	**Do you want a 2-minute break?**
Please put up your hand and wait	**Remember: wait quietly**
I am helping someone else, you must wait	**Have you asked _____ for help?**
Count to 20 very quietly, then I will help you	**Please go back to your seat**
STOP	**WAIT**

Schedules

Schedules provide an important tool to teach students with an autism spectrum disorder, as students have:

- limited understanding of the concept of time, i.e. knowing what is happening or will happen and then sequencing, predicting and organizing the order of events

- difficulty with communication, including difficulty understanding verbal explanations of what will happen at certain times during the day

- rigidity and a need for sameness – changes can create considerable stress for students with autism spectrum disorder. One way to reduce stress and increase opportunities for success is to use schedules.

A schedule is a tool that enables children to keep track of the day's events and activities, as well as develop an understanding of time frames and an appreciation of environmental sequences.

Schedules have the advantage of:

Increasing
independence
understanding
success
access to school curriculum
participation in school
   community

Decreasing
dependency on teacher or teacher's
   aide
dependency on verbal prompts
questioning
behavioural problems

Types of schedules

- Yearly diaries and timetables

- Term diaries

- Monthly calendars (see Figure 2)

- Weekly calendars and timetables

- Schedules of one hour, ten minutes or less

Month   Year

Sunday	Monday	Tuesday	Wednesday	Thursday	Friday	Saturday
				✕		
	C A M P —	—	—	—	—	→

Figure 2 Monthly calendar

Remember visuals

A variety of visuals are used in schedules. Remember, most students with autism spectrum disorder are visual learners, so where possible use pictures or written words in conjunction with verbal communication.

- Black and white line drawings

- Pictographs (e.g. COMPIC or Boardmaker)

- Written words

- Objects

- Remnants (part of an activity, e.g. a block from a train set)

- Photographs

- Comic strip illustrations

Three types of commonly used schedules

1. General daily classroom schedule with activities and individual tasks

2. Individual work skill schedule

3. Sequence charts or schedule of daily routines

How to use a schedule

A range of formats can be used, including posters, blackboard/whiteboard, diary, small photo albums, business card holders, cardboard strips or books.

Figure 3 Visual timetable for a classroom

Figure 4 Visual strategy to teach a routine

BEHAVIOUR

Schedules can be the cornerstone of management practices for children with challenging behaviours. Specific behavioural deficits can be managed using schedules, e.g. to clarify expectations, set limits or reduce negative teacher attention for undesired behaviour. Schedules can indicate that a preferred activity will follow a non-preferred activity.

COMMUNICATION

Schedules can be used in a large variety of ways to develop language and aid comprehension depending upon the individual student's needs. For students with limited verbal language, schedules can provide an opportunity to interact and communicate.

WRITING

For students who have difficulty writing stories, especially creative stories, schedules provide an excellent opportunity to develop written skills. Many students are motivated to write as they can relate to the text, and can have repeated opportunities to write about the day's events. This can be an excellent homework activity for students. (Examples of daily schedules are included on pp.24–25.)

MATHEMATICS

Schedules are excellent to use to teach time, numbers, days of the week, months and years – these are all important life skills. A calendar is included in the worksheets for the student to fill in the dates, events, month etc. The second daily schedule worksheet also provides an opportunity for the student to fill in 1st, 2nd, 3rd etc. You could also use clock stamps on a schedule to develop the ability to tell the time.

SOCIAL SKILLS

The playground can be an extremely challenging time for students with autism spectrum disorder and often the students find this an extremely overwhelming experience. Using a schedule of "activities to do in the playground" can considerably reduce anxiety. Provide a range of appropriate activities (using written words, pictographs or photos, depending upon students' needs). At first you may need to select the order.

Lunch Time: 1. Ball   2. Monkey Bars   3. Climbing

For students who have difficulty writing you could have the words or pictograph cut out, and they can either paste or attach them to the schedule.

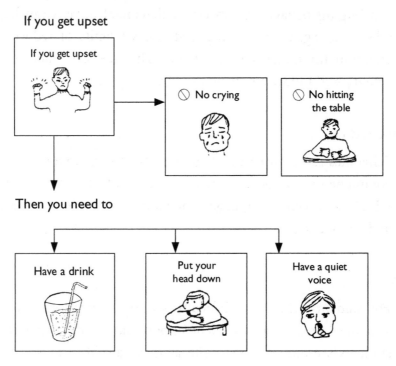

Figure 5 Schedule to help with social skills

SCHEDULES

On the following pages are a range of examples of schedules, which can be adapted to meet the individual student's needs.

Activity 1

The individual work schedule can be used to help the student work independently. It is recommended that you make a reusable page by laminating the schedule and making individual cards with words, pictures or photographs of objects related to scheduled tasks on the cards (for more information see "Schedules" on p.17). Put a picture or a word card in each box. As the student completes each task, he can either turn the card over or remove it. An example using pictographs is included in the worksheets.

Activity 2

Allow the student to have a choice of optional activities once he has completed the set activities. It is best if the student has chosen the reward before he starts the schedule of activities.

Activity 3

Two daily schedules are included that provide opportunities for writing. At first you may need to give the student a word list with the daily events. This is a great way to start the day for many students, as it provides an opportunity for them to sequence the day and process any changes. It can also be used as a homework activity of either reflecting on the day or preparing for the next day. You can make many variations on these worksheets. Space has been left on the second daily schedule for the student to complete 1st, 2nd, 3rd etc.

Activity 4

The blank monthly schedule can be used with photos of activities, people, events or words. It is recommended that the student completes this activity at the start of each month to help him develop a concept of time and anticipate events. You might include haircuts, camps, holidays, excursions, days when the teacher will be away, etc.

For some students, having one calendar at school that gets crossed off at the end of each day and another at home that gets crossed off before they go to bed is very useful. This helps them develop a concept of days, weeks and months which is an important life skill. Ultimately, aim to use a personal diary.

EXAMPLE INDIVIDUAL WORK SCHEDULE

1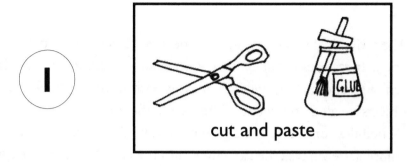
cut and paste

2
write

3
draw

4
finish

INDIVIDUAL WORK SCHEDULE

①

②

③

④

Today is
First I am going to
Next I will
Next I will
For recess I will eat
After recess I will
Next I will
Next I will
Then I will eat
At lunch time I will play
After lunch I will
Next I will
Next I will
Then I will go home with
At home I will

DAILY SCHEDULE 2

© Sue Larkey 2005

Today is_____

1 __ **We have** _____

2 __ **We will do** _____

3 __ **We will do** _____

4 __ **We will do** _____

5 __ **We will do** _____

6 __ **We will do** _____

7 __ **We will do** _____

8 __ **We will do** _____

✓

MONTHLY SCHEDULE

Month   Year

Sunday	Monday	Tuesday	Wednesday	Thursday	Friday	Saturday

PICTOGRAPHS

The benefit and purpose of pictographs is to provide a visual representation of a word or concept. Remember, most students with autism spectrum disorder are visual learners, so where possible use pictures or written words in conjunction with verbal communication. There are a number of pictograph/picture systems commercially available. Some computer-generated pictograph systems can be found on the web, for example Boardmaker and COMPIC. Some of these sites have examples you can download and try out.

How to use pictographs

- Use pictographs in schedules (like those provided in "Schedules" on p.17)

- Start with a few pictographs of everyday activities so the student can get used to using them regularly.

- Create a box or folder to keep the pictographs in, for easy access for teacher and student.

- Put the pictographs in small blank photo-books or business card holders for the student or teacher to access. Sometimes the student or teacher can wear this in a small waist bag.

- Use pictographs to increase the students understanding of what is required in different situations, for example "to wait" or "finish an activity."

- Pictographs often come in colour or black line drawings. Often it is worth checking which the student can understand, as sometimes the colour confuses students.

- Pictographs can be used as a communication system for the student, e.g. Picture Exchange Communication System (PECS).

- Include the written word under the pictographs as this will help the student's reading literacy skills.

- Make up games which use pictographs (e.g. Bingo, Memory, Matching).

- Have a system where the same pictographs are used at home, school and in the community to ensure generalisation (i.e. the student can use them in different places, not just one setting).

- Laminate the pictographs to help them last, and put velcro on the back. (This tends not to be removed like blu-tack and can be used over and over.)

- It is useful to make a couple of copies each symbol as they tend to get lost when used frequently.

Where to start

In schools the type of pictographs which are often the most useful are:

- routine concepts: lunch, recess (morning tea), home, toilet, play, eat, work

- activities : write, read, cut, paste, draw

- instructions: listen, wait, start, finish, quiet

- subjects: computers, exercise, maths, library, music, science, English.

Useful pictographs and symbols to make

RED CROSS

Cut strips of red paper and position on a card as seen below in Figure 6 then laminate the card. Red crosses are wonderful for reminding the student not to touch something. For example, they can be attached to door handles to stop the student running out of a room, or to computers, window openers, or car seat belts. Most students know this concept from the tick and cross system teachers use to indicate "correct" and "incorrect." This is also can lead to the community sign for "no."

Figure 6 Red cross

FINISH FLAG

Having a visual way to indicate an activity has finished is very important. The nature of autism spectrum disorder is such that students often do not know where to start or finish an activity. This is why we often see repetitive activities, where they do an activity over and over again, such as doing a puzzle, jumbling up the pieces, doing the puzzle again, etc. This is particularly seen with their

Figure 7 Finish

special interests where they may play an activity over and over and over and over or talk about the subject over and over and over. It is important to have a visual way to communicate that the activity or conversation has finished (they rarely respond to the verbal "finish" particularly when they are involved in an activity they love).

The "finish" pictograph can be made in a variety of sizes. A4 is particularly useful for putting over computer screens. Small business card sizes are great to put in business card holders (booklets with clear pages) and kept in a pocket for easy access.

Why use "finish" rather than "no"

Whenever possible avoid using the word "no" as students with Autism Spectrum tend to react dramatically to the word "no". It is preferable to use words or visuals like "Stop" or "Finish", or to tell the student what to do next, e.g. "Finished computer, time for puzzles." Using pictographs to support the words will also help the student move from one activity to the next. This is also a very useful behaviour strategy – sometimes when the student is doing inappropriate behaviours, indicating "finished" with a pictograph or signing "finished" will stop the behaviour.

Chapter 2

Successful Strategies for Group Instruction

The nature of autism spectrum disorder is such that the students have difficulties attending to the teacher during group instruction. These can include:

- difficulty understanding complex instructions (more than three steps)

- difficulty sitting in a group because of sensory difficulties as other students may touch the student and make movements or noises which may distract her from the teacher

- difficulty in sitting cross legged due to a range of sensory difficulties, for example they may not like the feel of the carpet or lino

- difficulty in understanding group instructions – in particular they do not tune in to the relevant instructions

- difficulty in understanding that to answer a group question they need to raise their hands: they call out answers as they believe the teacher is asking them a question directly – they do not understand it is a group question

- difficulty in waiting for a turn

- constantly asking questions (often irrelevant) or interrupting the teacher and other students.

Strategies

- Put a spot on the floor, which is where the student must always sit. If the floor surface distracts the student, get a square of fabric she likes for her to sit on (e.g. silk scarf, lino, fluffy fabric).

- Let the student sit on a chair behind the class so she doesn't have sensory difficulties.

- Use Social Stories to teach about group times (see "Social Stories" on p.47).

- Use the student's name to get her attention when you are about to give instructions.

- When giving instructions, have a visual cue (e.g. your hand in a fist) that indicates the student must listen carefully.

- Simplify your language and give instructions one step at a time.

- Have the instructions written out by the teacher aide or volunteer as you give them to the group.

- Use visual cues when possible, to explain a task, or write the steps on the board.

- Use a visual cue for when the student may answer a question (e.g. raise your hand when the student may speak).

- Use the pictographs for "wait a minute" and "quiet" to indicate visually to the student without interrupting the rest of the class. If you put them on the blackboard, the student's desk or a prominent place in the classroom, all you should need to do is point to them to remind the student not to interrupt.

- Give the student an object to hold in her hand to calm her. Excellent examples are tassels, pompoms, blu-tack and squeeze balls.

Additional activities to use

- Social Stories (e.g. "Putting up my hand" and "Sitting still") on p.49
- "Sensory activities" on p.103

Strategies for constant questioning

- Use the "quiet," "finish" or "wait" pictograph or sign language to remind the student not to interrupt.

- Tell the student she is allowed to ask three questions only. Give her three blocks to represent her questions and take one each time she asks a question.

- Tell the student she has already asked the question and use a business card holder or small photo album with a range of different questions the student can ask.

- Constant questioning is often the student's attempt at a conversation. Instead of answering in the same way, move the conversation on. For example, if the student says, "Do we have sport?", you could say, "Yes, at 10.15. Today we are doing soccer. Do you like soccer?"

- Tell the student that you have already answered the question and you will not answer the question again until a specific time, for example when she has finished eating all her lunch.

- Ignore the questions.

- Give a different answer every time or answer the question with a question. Many students just love the repetitive answers and getting the same answer is just wonderful, so change your answers. For example, if a student is constantly asking, "What time is sport?" answer, "10.15," "After Music," "Before Science," "Quarter past ten," "In the morning," etc.

- Some students really want to comment but have learnt that people ask questions of them all the time. Therefore they think it's appropriate to ask a question, even if they want to comment. Teach and model commenting by being attentive – nod and encourage comments.

CONVERSATION STARTERS

Instructions

Cut up the conversation starters on the worksheet and put them in a business card holder. Either the teacher or student can carry them. You will need to change them regularly and include questions of interest to the student.

CONVERSATION STARTERS

What did you do on the weekend?	**What is your favourite TV show?**
Do you have a family?	**What type of car do you drive?**
What is your favourite food?	**Have you seen any good movies lately?**
At what time do we have _____?	**Are we going on any trips this term?**

Chapter 3

Successful Strategies for Communication

The nature of autism spectrum disorder is such that students often:

- have no verbal communication; 50 per cent of students with autism do not develop verbal language

- acquire speech at an expected or mildly delayed age and tend to have a diagnosis of Asperger Syndrome

- display echololia: they repeat words or phrases they have heard from people or television – the variations are immediate echolalia (the adult asks, "How are you?" and the student replies, "How are you?") or delayed echolalia (the adult asks, "What is your name?" and the student says, "My name is Humpty Dumpty," from the song they heard on Playschool)

- use language which is rigid, formal or limited

- need visual support, e.g. signing or pictures to help them understand verbal language

- have difficulty understanding questions

- have a tendency to talk too much or too little.

Strategies

- The student often needs to develop an alternative form of communication to verbal language. This can include a range of systems. A speech therapist is best to consult to meet the student's individual needs.

- To increase the student's comprehension, a range of activities and games can be undertaken which require the student to listen (for examples see the worksheets in this chapter).

- Signing, pictographs, photos or gestures can be used by adults in conjunction with verbal language to enhance comprehension, e.g. instead of just saying, "Line up at the door," point to the door at the same time.

- For students who talk too much see "Strategies for constant questioning" on p.31.

WHAT AM I?

Aims

- For the student to answer the question "What?" in the context of "What am I?"

- For the student to listen to the clues and select an answer.

- For the student to play a game in a group.

- For the student to read the clues.

Instructions

Photocopy, laminate and cut up the clues. Keep the pictographs together as a group.

Activity 1

Place the pictographs so that the students can see them. Read out the clues and take turns to select the answers.

Activity 2

Let the students take it in turns to be the "teacher" and read out the clues.

Activity 3

Play the game without the pictograph clues.

Activity 4

Make up your own game. Get the students to write "What am I?" and draw a picture for the answer.

Variations

Who am I? Use photographs of known people (family, classmates, famous people from magazines). Laminate the photos and cut them down so that only the face and the hair are included. Clues can be "I have brown hair" etc.

Where am I? Include the student's favourite places, e.g. McDonalds.

WHAT AM I?

What am I? You wear me when it is cold. I have a zip and buttons. I keep you warm.	**What am I?** I carry your things. You bring me to school. You put your lunchbox in me.
What am I? I have fur. I have a tail and four legs. I say "Meow"	**What am I?** You have me when you are thirsty. I come in different flavours. You put me in a cup.
What am I? I am in your house. I have a wardrobe and bed in me. You sleep here.	**What am I?** I have 4 wheels. You put petrol in me. You drive me.

© Sue Larkey 2005

LANGUAGE ACTIVITIES

The House

Instructions

Copy the house scene onto a range of different coloured card (about 3 colours). Cut out the different objects, clouds etc. (This can be a cut and paste activity or made into a game by laminating etc.)

Activity 1

Start with two colours. Give the student instructions to follow. For example, "Put a yellow door on a blue house," "Put a yellow cloud above the house," "Put a blue cloud next to the yellow cloud."

Activity 2

Get the student to give an adult or another student instructions.

Activity 3

As a game with three or four students. Copy the sheet onto a range of colours (e.g. four colours if there are four students). Each student has a specific colour and the students have to ask each other for the colour they need e.g. "Anthony, can I please have a blue cloud?" Take turns to ask for different pieces to make a picture.

Farm Scene and Animals

These can be used in a similar way to the house scene. Laminate the farm animals in different colours and use the farm scene as the base sheet.

Game

Make two copies of the farm scene. Take turns to give instructions to create different farm scenes. Or put a barrier between the two players and both players follow the instructions. Compare pictures at the end.

THE HOUSE

© Sue Larkey 2005

FARM ANIMALS

FARM SCENE

COOKING

Cooking is a fantastic way to teach language, group skills and all the curriculum areas. In this example it is used to develop language and group skills. Western Autistic School has devised a cookbook called *Look, Cook and Learn*, from which two recipes are included.

Aims

- For the student to follow instructions.
- For the student to give instructions to other students.
- For the student to take turns.
- For the student to wait quietly for a turn.

Activity 1

An adult gives the student verbal instructions to get specific ingredients and follow the recipe.

Activity 2

The student reads the recipe and follows the instructions.

Activity 3

The student is responsible for following the recipe and giving instructions to other students.

Further ideas

- Cut up the recipe and get the student to put the steps in order.
- Get the student to write out instructions for a recipe.
- Make your own class cookbook.
- Take photos of cooking and make your own storybook.
- Take photos of three or four distinct stages of cooking (e.g. putting on an apron, getting ingredients, eating). Get the student to put them in order and tell a story from the sequence.

PIKELETS RECIPE

Ingredients

self-raising flour

butter

milk

sugar

egg

Utensils

bowl

cup

spoon

frying pan

egg lifter

Instructions

- Put 1 cup of flour in the bowl.
- Add 2 tablespoons of sugar.
- Add 1 egg and mix.
- Add ½ cup of milk and mix.
- Sultanas or chocolate chips may be added.
- Turn on the frying pan to medium heat.
- Put 1 tablespoon of butter in the frying pan.
- Drop spoonfuls of the mixture into the pan.
- Cook gently until bubbles appear on the top.
- Turn over and cook on the other side.

FRENCH TOAST RECIPE

Get egg   bowl

Break 1 egg into the bowl

Get milk  cup

spoon

Add ¼ cup of milk and mix with spoon

Get a frying pan

Turn the frying pan on to a medium heat

Get butter tablespoon

Put 2 tablespoons of butter into the frying pan

Get bread

Adapted from *Look, Cook and Learn*, Western Autistic School, with permisson.

Put a slice of bread in the milk and egg mixture

Cook the bread in the frying pan

Get the egg lifter

Turn the bread with the egg lifter

Get a plate

Lift out the toast with the egg lifter and put toast on the plate

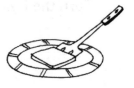

Signing

Signing can be an important form of communication for students with autism spectrum disorder, especially students with limited language or understanding of language. People with autism spectrum disorder, like Temple Grandin, tell us that when they were young they thought adults spoke a different language to each other. We often see this with children with autism spectrum disorder where they seem to not hear us. This is a very important reason to use signing as it facilitates the student's understanding. Signing ensures everyone uses the same gesture, therefore not confusing the student.

Generally students do not need to use signing to communicate with the adult. The adult signs to help the student understand what other people are saying. For example, if a student is standing up at mat time you might sign "sit" while saying, "Sit on the mat." Or if a student is frustrated because he can't open his bag, you may sign "help" whilst saying, "You want help to open the bag," or simply sign "help" to remind him to ask you for help.

Use the sign language that is known in your country. The most commonly used signs are:

- wait
- help
- finish
- toilet
- stop
- drink
- eat
- work
- stand up
- sit down
- play
- outside
- inside
- music
- good.

Chapter 4
Successful Strategies for Social Skills

The nature of autism spectrum disorder is such that students often:

- lack the ability to understand the rules of social behaviour
- exhibit unusual eye contact or no eye contact
- are aware of their social problems but do not know appropriate ways to overcome them
- want friends but are unsure how to develop or maintain friendships – friendships often burn out quickly
- have no intuitive knowledge of how to adapt to the needs and personalities of others
- lack the ability to understand the consequences of their behaviour
- rote learn social skills with no adaptability
- are unaware of others' feelings and reactions
- indulge in lengthy monologues about their special interests or continually repeat some questions, conversations or phrases
- have poor conversational skills (unable to take turns in conversation, or change topics)
- exhibit little or learnt facial expressions except for strong emotions (e.g. anger)
- use unusual gestures
- misinterpret other people's body language (e.g. may continue to do a behaviour even if given an angry facial expression by another person)
- talk too much or talk too little
- use formal, idiosyncratic, pedantic, precocious speech.

Strategies

- Social Stories, which explain to the student how to interact in specific situations, are very useful (see the following section).

- Games, which include specific rules, can be used to teach turn taking, waiting, listening, rules and sitting quietly. Board games like Trouble, Snakes and Ladders (there is a Thomas the Tank Engine Snakes and Ladders available for those who have a special interest)

- Use activities the student is motivated by to encourage social interaction, in a natural situation. For example, if a student is an excellent speller let him be the class "dictionary" and help other students. If the student likes chess, start a school chess club so he can learn social interaction within the context of an activity.

- Teach the student to ask other students for help and interact with classmates rather than always going to the teacher first. Use the card "Have you asked _____for help?" (insert student's name) to encourage the interaction.

Social Stories

Carol Gray developed the concept of Social Stories™ for students with autism spectrum disorder (see Useful Resources on p.117). The aim of Social Stories is to develop social understanding. It is important when introducing a Social Story that it is introduced in a relaxed, positive environment where the student can "learn" the social situation and develop an understanding of the social context. Carol Gray strongly believes telling them during a misbehaviour or as a consequence of a behaviour is inappropriate. They are a teaching tool!

Some examples of how to use Social Stories include making a book, putting them on reminder cards or making them into a comic strip. Ensure the student reads the story with a range of people to reinforce it.

One of the key learnings from the concept of Social Stories is how confusing a social situation can be for a student. Social situations are constantly changing and this can be extremely frustrating for the student, especially when he does not have the skills to interpret the change of social rules.

The following examples are from *Annette Joosten's Book of Cool Strategies*[1] which was derived from stories created for students attending special education

---

1   *Annette Joosten's Book of Cool Strategies: A Personal Social Script Workbook for Australian Primary-age Students* by Annette Joosten. Pilot Ed 2003. Book in Hand, Brisbane, Australia. Order from www.bookinhand.com.au or 1800 505 221.

settings and mainstream schools in Australia. They are particularly suitable for people on the autistic spectrum but can be used with a much wider population.

The 41 scripts may be used as 'templates' and developed to suit different students. The book can also be issued to an individual student and personalised to his needs. Each script has an "Additional Workpage for this Story" on the facing page to allow for added sentences, symbols, drawings, photographs, etc. Unwanted or unsuitable stories can be detached before use without damage to the binding.

For example, two "Lining up" scripts are included here. One of these was devised for a child who was sometimes restless in line and tended to touch others. The other was for a child who found that being in line was a difficult experience because other students might touch him. If one story is not required, it may be removed from the student workbook.

Annette emphasizes that these stories:

- should be part of overall support of the child's behaviour

- need to be introduced with the support of an adult to ensure comprehension

- should be read to, or available for the child to read, at any time

- may require you to cue the child to think about his story or read the story, either before or after a target situation

- may need modifying – observe the child's response to determine if this is necessary

- may have immediate or gradual effects and this may be dependent on the frequency of opportunities to read the stories

- can be faded out or adapted as the child's understanding and behaviour changes.

Lining up 1

After recess and lunch the bell rings. When the bell rings we need to line up to go back into class. Lining up means going to stand outside my classroom with the other children in my class.

We stand in line. Someone will usually be in front of me and someone will usually be behind me. When we stand in line I try not to touch anyone. I try to stand still and quiet. When the teacher comes he or she will tell us when to go into class. My teacher is happy when I line up with my class.

Lining up 2

We line up to come into class. Sometimes children bump into me when we line up. I try to stay calm if they bump into me. If they keep bumping or touching me I can tell the teacher.

Sometimes I can be first in line. Sometimes someone else might be first in line. Sometimes I can stand last in line. I might not get bumped when I am last in line. There will be no one behind me when I am last in line.

Putting up my hand

One rule in my class is that we must put our hands up and not call out when we want the teacher's attention. I can put my hand up to ask the teacher a question. I can put my hand up to answer the teacher's question. I do not put my hand up if I do not know the answer to the teacher's question. I can put my hand up if I need to ask the teacher to go to the toilet.

There are many children in my class – it is too noisy if we call out to the teacher. We must put our hand up when we want the teacher's attention. The teacher is happy when I follow the rule and put my hand up in class.

Staying with the group

Sometimes my class has to move to another part of the school. When my class goes out of my room the teacher tells us where we have to go and to stay with the group. Staying with the group means we all walk together. When we walk together the teacher knows where everyone is and no one will be late. The teacher is happy when I stay with the group.

Sitting still

Sometimes my teacher will say "Sit still." Sitting still means: I will keep my legs still; I will try to keep my hands on my lap; I will try not to touch other children. The teacher is happy when I sit still.

Everyone gets angry

Everyone gets angry sometimes. It is OK to be angry. When I get angry I try to control my anger. I take a deep breath. I count to five. I move away from the person making me angry. I feel good when I can control my anger.

Games

The following are examples of how to use a range of games to encourage social skills.

Ball games

Roll or throw the ball and get the students to look at another student and say his name before passing the ball.

Tray of missing objects

Put up to seven objects on a tray. Cover the tray with a cloth and remove object(s). Get the students to put up their hands to say what is missing. Let a student be the teacher and ask one of the students with his hand up what is missing.

Party games

- Musical chairs
- Pass the parcel
- Egg and spoon race
- Pin the tail on the donkey
- Who stole the cookie from the cookie jar?
- Drop the hankie
- Three legged race

Books

For students with autism spectrum disorder who enjoy reading and stories, books can be used as a way to encourage social interaction with the class.

- Get the student to read a book to the class.
- Get the student to read a book with a group of students, taking turns to read a page.
- Get a group of students to act out a story. This will involve taking turns and interacting with other students.
- Find a book with actions and get a group of students to learn the actions and teach the rest of the class.
- Put on a puppet play using a story, e.g. Wombat Stew.

Asking and answering questions

Make a game about asking questions. In a bag put a range of questions, take turns with the student to ask and answer the questions…then get other children to join in. Or why not make it for the whole class!

Be very careful when writing the questions as many students with autism spectrum disorder find questions extremely threatening. Remember to keep them visual.

Example questions

Easily prompted answers:

- What colour are your shoes?

- What colour are your trousers?

- Who is your teacher?

Answers requiring memory or greater understanding:

- What is your name?

- How old are you?

- When is your birthday?

- How many people in your family?

- Do you have any pets?

- What is your favourite TV programme?

- How do you get to school?

- What time do you go to bed?

You could also see if the student could think of some questions.

Chapter 5

Successful Strategies for English

The nature of autism spectrum disorder is such that in English the students may have:

- difficulty writing due to problems with fine motor control; see "Fine motor activities" on p.54

- difficulty writing imaginative stories on a range of topics

- difficulty recalling set tasks and difficulty starting a writing activity

- a preference for "non-fiction" activities where they can gather knowledge and facts

- have "hyperlexia," the ability to read text, but not a matching comprehension of text

- an extensive vocabulary, however, their understanding of language is concrete and literal

- difficulty understanding questions

- fear of taking risks with topics and only like writing when they can spell the words perfectly or write letters perfectly (including writing the letter "a" like the typed "a")

- a preference for writing in capital letters and rarely use lower case (this is an autism phenomenon; there are a number of theories why this happens, but no definite facts).

Strategies

Writing

- Co-actively write, putting your hand over the top of the student's.

- Use a computer for the student to write.

- Use a tape recorder for the student to record his work.

- Use a voice activated computer which transcribes for the student. (Dragon Program is very good. If you don't have access to the money for a computer, it is always worth trying to apply to the Variety Club or other charities.)

- Implement a fine motor programme to develop strength in his fingers. (See "Fine motor activities" on p.54.)

- Teach the student how to use a dictionary to look up words to spell, or start his own dictionary.

- Show the student that you make mistakes, and what you do when you make a mistake (i.e. cross out the word once).

- If the student writes in capitals, it needs to be clear if this is perceived as a problem. However, if your aim is for the student to write a story and he completes the task, does it matter if it is in capitals?

- Stick his book or page to the desk so he doesn't have to hold the page.

- Raise the writing surface up to an angle using a board and blocks.

Writing stories

- Let the student write about "real things" that happened to him (e.g. Christmas Day), and use this as the basis for creative writing (e.g. ask "What would have happened if…there were no presents?…the turkey burnt?").

- To help the student with ideas, use a small photo album with pictures to stimulate stories. Ask the family to send in photos of family events for the student to write about or cut pictures out of magazines.

- Tell the student exactly how many sentences or pages you want in the story. You could even put a start and finish dot on a page for him, or give him a word limit.

- Write the first sentence for him (as starting is often the problem).

- Use "sentence starters" in an envelope, which he can take one of to help him get started.

- Photocopy a book the class has read and cut up the sentences and get the student to paste them in the correct order.

- Scribe the student's story and cut it up. Then get him to put the parts in order.

Reading

- Read stories that include the student's special interests to motivate reading and comprehension.

- Include mainly non-fiction books rather than fiction.

- Make photo books about his own experiences to encourage reading. Paste a photo on a page and get the student to tell you the story, type it on the computer and then laminate and bind as a personal book. Families often have lots of spare photos or take a roll of film of the student at school.

- To extend comprehension remind the student to look at the pictures.

- Ask questions to check comprehension.

- If the student has difficulty with questions start a sentence "The boy is…" rather than "What is the boy doing?"

- If the student enjoys drawing, get him to draw pictures about the text he has read.

- Use cut and paste activities. For example, cut up the sentences and have the student match the words to pictographs.

IMPORTANT POINT WHEN TEACHING READING

As the majority of students with autism spectrum disorder are visual learners, they generally respond best to visual approaches to learning new words, or a "whole word" approach. Sometimes phonetic based approaches delay acquisition of reading or only teach "sounding out" rather than reading.

Additional worksheets to use

- Schedules (see worksheets on pp.22–26)

Fine motor activities

Activities

- Playdough and clay.

- Threading – use a range of different strings for threading activities: shoe laces, strong plastic threads, fishing line, string, wool.

- Squeezing a range of objects and balls.

- Peg activities – pegging onto a toy washing line; pegging onto an ice cream container; cards with different colours for matching to coloured pegs; pegging the student's art onto a painting frame.

- Shaving cream: get the student to draw a picture on a table or move their figures in different ways – tapping, squeezing, opening/shutting fingers.

- Finger paint.

- Make necklaces or bracelets out of pasta, beads or cut-up straws.

- Push toothpicks into foam, clay or playdough.

- Wind-up toys (e.g. cars, music boxes).

- Rubber band activities on geo boards, around blocks, around margarine containers or onto strong cardboard, matching the colour of the rubber band to the colour of the cardboard.

- Lego and Duplo activities – both putting together and pulling apart.

- Opening and closing a range of jars, containers and purses.

- Dressing activities for himself or a doll with different zips and fasteners.

- Lock Boards with different locks can be very motivating (check your local toy library for one).

- Finger puppet or hand puppet plays.

- Putting money in a money box or a container with different size slots.

- Construction activities.

- Nuts and bolts – they can match and screw together.

Cutting

- Co-actively cut.

- Demonstrate cutting.

- Hold the paper so the student can just focus on cutting, then co-actively cut.

- Use stronger paper so it is easier to hold.

- Draw a bigger shape around a picture of their special interest, e.g. a big square around a picture of a bus.

- Cutting activities that have a purpose or motivation for the student, e.g. making a shape or object of special interest.

- Snipping the edge of the paper to make a fringe.

- Cutting straight lines, then curves.

- Cut out the first half of the picture.

- Always have a spare (same activity) as cutting can be very frustrating for some students.

An occupational therapist could devise a specific fine motor programme for the student.

DRAWING

In the first group of instructions, tasks are set out line by line for students who have difficulty returning to the place they have read up to after completing an instruction. In the second group the layout is more complex as tasks are set in one continuous paragraph.

Aims

- For the student to follow written instructions.

- To test the student's comprehension of written words.

- For the student to draw a broader range of pictures.

- For the student to make choices between two or three activities.

- For the student to work independently at his desk.

Activity I

- Cut out the instructions and make them into laminated cards that can be used again.

- Give the student two to four cards depending upon his ability at making choices. Let him choose which picture he will draw or the order he will do the activities.

Activity 2

- Cut out the instructions and paste them on a page as a worksheet.

- Put a dot or cross on the page to indicate where the student should start the drawing.

You can write many more of these if the student enjoys them. They are excellent for spare time or calming for many students. Remember to make them experiences to which the student will be able to relate.

DRAWING

The Library

Draw a boy reading a book.
Colour his clothes blue.
Draw a bookshelf.
Draw a table and chair.

The Park

Draw a slide.
Draw a swing next to the slide.
Draw a boy on the swing.
Draw a tree in the park.
Draw a bird in the tree.

Balloons

Draw six balloons.
Colour one balloon red.
Colour two balloons blue.
Colour three balloons green.

Swimming Pool

Draw a swimming pool.
Draw children playing
in the swimming pool.
Draw a diving board.
Colour in the picture.

The Road

Draw a road. Draw a truck on the road. Draw a red car on the
road. Draw a stop sign. Colour in the picture using yellow, red,

The Park

Draw a park with a big pond. Draw eight ducks on the pond.
Draw a lady feeding the ducks. Draw trees in the park.

The City

Draw the city. Draw a train going to the city. Draw a boy in the
city. Colour in the picture.

STAMPS AND CUT OUTS

Aims

- To teach the concepts of "in between," "on top of" and "under."
- For the student to follow written instructions.
- For fine motor activity of stamping on the page using a tripod grip.

Activity 1

1. For the two stamp worksheets, use a number of different stamps, e.g. animals, smily face, Christmas, coin, shapes, etc.

2. Put different stamps in each of the boxes provided on the worksheets.

3. Fill in the blank lines in the text.

4. Get the student to follow the directions and put the stamps on the worksheets by following the instructions.

Activity 2

This relates to the cut outs worksheet. Photocopy the worksheet and get the student to cut out the animal pictographs and paste them on another sheet of paper according to the instructions. You can make the cut outs reusable by photocopying the worksheet onto card and laminating it before cutting out the animal pictographs. Put blu-tack on the back of the cut outs so that they can be attached to cardboard.

Further activities

- Use real objects. Use either written or verbal instructions and get the student to follow (e.g. "Put the duck in the bowl," "Put the duck under the bowl").
- Make it into a group game. Let one student be the "teacher" and direct other students to follow directions (using either the reusable activity or real objects).

STAMPS 1

Stamp the _____ in between the _____ and the _____

Stamp the _____ on top of the _____

Stamp the _____ under the _____

STAMPS 2

Stamp the _____ under the _____

Stamp the _____ on top of the _____

Stamp the _____ next to the _____

CUT OUTS

Paste the sheep *next to* the snail

Paste the rabbit *under* the snail

Paste the pig *on top of* the snail

pig

rabbit

sheep

snail

DAYS AND MONTHS

Aims

- For the student to cut and paste.
- For the student to match words.
- For the student to order the days and months.
- For the student to learn to write the days and months.
- For the student to type on the computer.

Activity 1

Make two copies of the worksheet. Get the student to cut up one sheet and place the cut-up days and months in the same order as they are on the second sheet.

Activity 2

Give the student one copy to cut and paste onto a separate sheet.

The teacher should select a different day or month to start so the student can learn the order starting at different days and months.

Activity 3

Copy the sheet and get the student to write the words next to the typing.

Activity 4

Get the student to type the list on the computer.

Activity 5

Get the student to write significant events that happen on each day and month. For example, physical education is on Monday. In the months they could write other students' or family members' birthdays.

Activity 6

Make a reusable activity by copying the page on card. Make a cut-up copy with blu-tack or velcro on the back of the cards to attach to cardboard.

January
February
March
April
May
June
July
August
September
October
November
December

Monday
Tuesday
Wednesday
Thursday
Friday
Saturday
Sunday

WRITING

There are many commercial books available for writing activities. Try to choose worksheets which are not too busy, and include the words or pictures to help the student. The following are examples of simple, clear worksheets that allow the student to practise writing and not be distracted by busy worksheets.

Aims

- For the student to write words.

- For the student to complete worksheets independently.

- For the student to select items they can see in the classroom and record.

Activity 1

On the first "I can see" worksheet, the student can select the word for each pictograph from the bottom of the worksheet and write it next to the pictograph. For the second "I can see" worksheet, the student needs to look around the room and select objects or people and write them in the spaces provided.

Activity 2

Using the "I like to eat" worksheet, the student needs to decide which of the items at the bottom of the sheet are edible and write the word in the space provided. For students who have difficulty writing, this worksheet can be used by cutting out the pictographs and pasting them in space provided.

FURTHER ACTIVITIES

As a future life skill, filling in forms is very important. You can collect lots of different forms and copy them so the students get used to filling in their names, contact details and other information on different types of form (e.g. Medicare forms, enrolment forms).

"I CAN SEE" 1

I can see	
I can see	
I can see	
I can see	
I can see	
I can see	
I can see	

drink   duck   fish   orange juice

milk   cow   bird

"I CAN SEE" 2

I can see
I can see
I can see
I can see
I can see
I can see
I can see

"I LIKE TO EAT"

I like to eat
I like to eat
I like to eat
I like to eat
I like to eat

apple banana biscuit dog

jumper shoes bus car

cat chips chocolate fruit

Chapter 6

Successful Strategies for Mathematics

The nature of autism spectrum disorder is such that students often:

- have a strength in mathematics

- have a special interest or obsession in mathematics

- like the rigidity of mathematics and want to ask the same questions over and over to get the same response

- have difficulty understanding the "language" of mathematics as many words are interchangeable (e.g. times and multiply)

- have difficulties with problem solving and understanding abstract concepts

- have difficulty comprehending space concepts, e.g. near and far

- don't generalize their knowledge – examples of this are autistic savants who know how to calculate football scores in a second, but can't add two numbers, or students who can add up money at school, but can't in a shop.

Strategies

- Use the student's interest in mathematics to develop a range of skills.

- Set a clear rule on how many times she can ask the same question. Use ticks on the board to indicate each time she asks the question as a reminder.

- Use real life examples to help her understand the language of mathematics.

- Develop a mathematics dictionary which helps her understand the concepts by including examples.

Additional activities to use

- Computer activities on pp.89–90

ADDITION AND SUBTRACTION SHEETS AND CALCULATOR ACTIVITIES

Aims

- For the student to complete mathematics equations.

- For the student to learn the language of mathematics: addition or plus, subtraction or minus, equals or makes, equations, problems etc.

- For the student to complete worksheets independently.

- For the student to use a calculator to check answers to equations.

Instructions

To enable the student to learn a range of mathematical language, space has been left at the top of the worksheets for you to write in the instructions at the individual student's level. The worksheets can be enlarged to A4 or the appropriate font size for the student. It is recommended that the student completes the worksheets a number of times to see her increasing success or for relaxation. Vary the instructions to improve her understanding of mathematical terms. To increase the student's motivation, put a picture of her special interest on the sheet.

There are many great mathematics resource books available. The following worksheets are just a few ideas to get you started. Ensure the worksheets you find in other resources are not overcrowded and use language the student understands.

Activitiy 1

Time the student to race to the finish.

Activity 2

Have the child check answers with a calculator.

Activity 3

Use dice to make their own sums.

ADDITION 1

Instructions:

1. $4 + 5 =$	11. $7 + 3 =$
2. $4 + 4 =$	12. $1 + 4 =$
3. $4 + 6 =$	13. $8 + 2 =$
4. $8 + 4 =$	14. $6 + 6 =$
5. $3 + 4 =$	15. $3 + 9 =$
6. $5 + 5 =$	16. $2 + 1 =$
7. $6 + 7 =$	17. $3 + 9 =$
8. $2 + 4 =$	18. $8 + 6 =$
9. $5 + 7 =$	19. $5 + 7 =$
10. $8 + 1 =$	20. $2 + 6 =$

ADDITION 2

Instructions:

1. $3 + 7 =$	11. $7 + 4 =$
2. $5 + 10 =$	12. $3 + 12 =$
3. $4 + 6 =$	13. $9 + 4 =$
4. $6 + 9 =$	14. $10 + 5 =$
5. $2 + 8 =$	15. $4 + 2 =$
6. $8 + 7 =$	16. $4 + 12 =$
7. $6 + 4 =$	17. $6 + 10 =$
8. $1 + 9 =$	18. $9 + 6 =$
9. $4 + 11 =$	19. $11 + 4 =$
10. $5 + 5 =$	20. $3 + 12 =$

22. Write all the sums that add up to make 15

21. Write all the sums that add up to make 10

ADDITION 3

Instuctions:

1.	2 + 11 =	12.	32 + 33 =
2.	12 + 25 =	13.	38 + 41 =
3.	25 + 4 =	14.	65 + 22 =
4.	5 + 16 =	15.	39 + 40 =
5.	32 + 62 =	16.	71 + 9 =
6.	2 + 51 =	17.	18 + 67 =
7.	38 + 31 =	18.	54 + 4 =
8.	61 + 7 =	19.	69 + 21 =
9.	43 + 21 =	20.	43 + 15 =
10.	87 + 11 =	21.	18 + 23 =

ADDITION 4

Instuctions:

1.	5 + 5 + 5 =	11.	4 + 2 + 2 =
2.	4 + 4 + 4 =	12.	3 + 7 + 4 =
3.	5 + 3 + 5 =	13.	2 + 8 + 9 =
4.	6 + 4 + 3 =	14.	4 + 7 + 3 =
5.	6 + 8 + 2 =	15.	5 + 2 + 2 =
6.	9 + 4 + 3 =	16.	3 + 5 + 9 =
7.	7 + 5 + 2 =	17.	7 + 3 + 8 =
8.	2 + 4 + 5 =	18.	4 + 4 + 5 =
9.	8 + 2 + 4 =	19.	7 + 2 + 4 =
10.	3 + 4 + 7 =	20.	6 + 4 + 7 =

ROLL DICE TO MAKE UP YOUR OWN SUMS

Instructions:

1.	+	=		11.	+	=
2.	+	=		12.	+	=
3.	+	=		13.	+	=
4.	+	=		14.	+	=
5.	+	=		15.	+	=
6.	+	=		16.	+	=
7.	+	=		17.	+	=
8.	+	=		18.	+	=
9.	+	=		19.	+	=
10.	+	=		20.	+	=

SUBTRACTION I

Instructions:

1.	$10 - 5 =$		11.	$12 - 4 =$
2.	$9 - 4 =$		12.	$14 - 5 =$
3.	$11 - 1 =$		13.	$11 - 2 =$
4.	$14 - 6 =$		14.	$17 - 9 =$
5.	$15 - 3 =$		15.	$13 - 5 =$
6.	$18 - 8 =$		16.	$15 - 7 =$
7.	$13 - 5 =$		17.	$18 - 2 =$
8.	$15 - 1 =$		18.	$15 - 6 =$
9.	$17 - 3 =$		19.	$11 - 4 =$
10.	$19 - 7 =$		20.	$12 - 8 =$

SUBTRACTION 2

Instructions:

1.	15 – 5 =	11.	12 – 2 =
2.	20 – 5 =	12.	17 – 2 =
3.	15 – 1 =	13.	20 – 10 =
4.	16 – 6 =	14.	13 – 3 =
5.	17 – 6 =	15.	18 – 3 =
6.	11 – 1 =	16.	19 – 9 =
7.	19 – 4 =	17.	14 – 4 =
8.	13 – 2 =	18.	20 – 5 =
9.	17 – 7 =	19.	18 – 8 =
10.	18 – 7 =	20.	14 – 7 =

SUBTRACTION 3

Instructions:

1.	20 – 5 =	11.	32 – 12 =
2.	15 – 5 =	12.	30 – 15 =
3.	35 – 15 =	13.	22 – 12 =
4.	28 – 8 =	14.	23 – 8 =
5.	26 – 16 =	15.	27 – 7 =
6.	26 – 11 =	16.	25 – 10 =
7.	35 – 5 =	17.	28 – 8 =
8.	25 – 10 =	18.	40 – 20 =
9.	30 – 8 =	19.	20 – 5 =
10.	50 – 25 =	20.	30 – 15 =

21. Write all the sums that subtract to make 10

22. Write all the sums that subtract to make 15

CALCULATOR PRACTICE: ADDITION

Instructions:

1.	5 + 10 = 15	11.	11 + 8 = 19
2.	10 + 10 = 20	12.	7 + 7 = 14
3.	6 + 6 = 12	13.	16 + 4 = 20
4.	15 + 15 = 30	14.	11 + 11 = 22
5.	2 + 8 = 10	15.	8 + 7 = 15
6.	8 + 8 = 16	16.	5 + 10 = 15
7.	18 + 2 = 20	17.	9 + 9 = 18
8.	3 + 7 = 10	18.	13 + 13 = 26
9.	18 + 12 = 30	19.	9 + 6 = 15
10.	16 + 9 = 25	20.	12 + 12 = 24

CALCULATOR PRACTICE: SUBTRACTION

Instructions:

1.	15 − 5 = 10	11.	35 − 20 = 15
2.	20 − 5 = 15	12.	14 − 7 = 7
3.	16 − 6 = 10	13.	10 − 5 = 5
4.	30 − 5 = 25	14.	15 − 9 = 6
5.	18 − 3 = 15	15.	16 − 8 = 8
6.	22 − 11 = 11	16.	24 − 14 = 10
7.	32 − 16 = 16	17.	22 − 12 = 10
8.	18 − 9 = 9	18.	12 − 6 = 6
9.	10 − 6 = 4	19.	28 − 8 = 20
10.	15 − 5 = 10	20.	50 − 25 = 25

WORD AND NUMERAL ACTIVITIES

Aims

- For the student to match the numerals and words.

- For the student to recognize the written word for numerals.

- For the student to match the word to the numeral.

- For the student to match the numeral to the word.

- For the student to write the words of numbers.

- For the student to complete cut and paste activities.

Instructions

The word and numeral grids can be interchanged and used in different combinations for individual students' needs. Once the student can complete to the number 10, you can make the same activity up to the number 20 etc.

Activity 1

Photocopy the worksheet on p.76 and cut out the words and numerals from the first two grids. Get the student to match the words to the corresponding numerals. If the student is frustrated because the cards keep moving, use blu-tack on the back of the cards to hold them in place.

Activity 2

Get the student to put the numerals in order and then the words in order.

Activity 3

Make another photocopy of the worksheet and get the student to paste the cut out words on top of the corresponding numerals on the first grid, then paste the cut out numerals on top of the corresponding words on the second grid.

Activity 4

Have the student complete the written words in the third grid.

Activity 5

Get the student to fill in the missing numbers in the worksheet on p.77.

Activity 6

Get the student to fill in each empty space in the worksheets on pp.78–79 by adding the number at the top of the column to the number at the beginning of the row.

WORD AND NUMERAL GRIDS

1	2	3	4	5
6	7	8	9	10

One	Two	Three	Four	Five
Six	Seven	Eight	Nine	Ten

O__	T__	T__	F__	F__
S__	S__	E__	N__	T__

NUMERAL GRIDS I

1	2	3	4	__	6	7	8	__	10
11	12	__	14	15	__	17	__	19	20

1	2	__	4	5	__	7	__	9	10
11	__	13	14	15	__	17	__	19	__

__	2	__	4	5	6	__	8	__	10
__	12	__	14	15	__	17	18	__	20

1	__	3	__	5	__	7	__	9	__
11	__	13	__	15	__	17	__	19	__

NUMERAL GRIDS 2

	0	1	2	3	4
0					
1					
2					
3					
4					

	0	1	2	3	4	5	6	7
0								
1								
2								
3								
4								
5								
6								
7								

NUMERAL GRID 3

Name _____

	0	1	2	3	4	5	6	7	8	9	10
0											
1											
2											
3											
4											
5											
6											
7											
8											
9											
10											

MONEY

Aims

- For the student to recognize coins.

- For the student to distinguish between different values of coins.

- For the student to add coin amounts together.

Activity 1

The coin worksheet with a range of coin images on it can be used in a variety of ways:

- Match real coins to the coin images.

- Colour coins different colours, e.g. colour the 5 cents blue and the 10 cents red.

- Count how many there are of each coin.

- Make two copies of the page. Cut out the coins from one sheet and paste them onto the matching coins on the other sheet.

- Add up the value of all the coins on the page.

Activity 2

Add the value of coins together.

Activity 3

- Using the money grid worksheet, get the student to add the different values together so she can see the patterns.

- Use real money in the grid squares to practise with real money.

Further activities

- Shopping games can include the amount (image or real coin) attached to the item to make it easier.

- Shopping games where the student only has one of each coin in her purse and the items are priced so that they have to find the two coins, e.g. 25 cents.

- Use shopping catalogues and get the student to find what she can buy for $2, $5 etc.

- Use shopping catalogues and get the student to use coin stamps to indicate which coins she would need to buy an item.

- Coin stamp activities (many students love the stamps; however, do ensure they are as competent with real money).

COINS

MONEY GRID

	5 CENTS	10 CENTS	20 CENTS	1 DOLLAR	2 DOLLAR
5 CENTS					
10 CENTS					
20 CENTS					
50 CENTS					
1 DOLLAR					
2 DOLLAR					

TV GUIDE

Television can be a particularly motivating activity for students, as many love TV because it is predictable and has repetitive commercials etc. Some families experience great stress when regular favourites are taken off over the summer!

Aims

- For the student to gather information from a larger text.

- For the student to complete a written activity that develops the mathematical concept of time.

- For the student to transfer information she has read onto a worksheet.

Instructions

Get a TV guide, or ask the parents to bring in one that the student uses at home. This worksheet repeats the same task three times. You might need to demonstrate the first time.

SHOPPING CATALOGUE

Instructions

Many students love shopping catalogues. Once again ask the parents to send in the student's favourite catalogues. There is space on the worksheet for you to fill in the items to find. You can repeat this worksheet with a range of catalogues or get the student to fill in the items herself.

The final section of the worksheet, to select two items, can be extremely difficult for the student, as choosing can be confusing. You may need to narrow this to a specific page.

Role model

For example you might actually model to the student how to do the worksheet. YES, you do the whole worksheet and then give her a copy. You might be surprised at the result – especially if your aim is for the student to sit quietly and complete an activity independently.

TV GUIDE

NAME _____

Neighbours is on Channel _____ at _____

Wheel of Fortune is on Channel _____ at _____

Sale of the New Century is on Channel _____ at _____

After the News on Channel 9 is _____

After Sale of the New Century on Channel 9 is _____

After the News on Channel 2 is _____

On Channel 10 at 4.00pm you can watch _____

On Channel 2 at 8.30pm you can watch _____

On Channel 2 at 5.00pm you can watch _____

SHOPPING CATALOGUE

The _____ costs $ ____ . ____

The _____ costs $ ____ . ____

The _____ costs $ ____ . ____

The _____ costs $ ____ . ____

The _____ costs $ ____ . ____

The _____ costs $ ____ . ____

The _____ costs $ ____ . ____

The _____ costs $ ____ . ____

The _____ costs $ ____ . ____

The _____ costs $ ____ . ____

Cut out two things you would like to buy.

Paste them in the boxes.

Chapter 7

Successful Strategies for Computers

Computers provide an important tool to teach students with an autism spectrum disorder as they allow us to present information tailored to students' unique learning styles.

Benefits of using computers

Learning style

Students with autism are visual learners. By using computers we can support verbal instruction with a visual presentation.

Opportunity to practise skills

Computers provide predictable routines, information and responses, which is ideally suited to students with autism spectrum disorder. As the computer provides the same response every time a sequence of steps is followed, this can give the student greater opportunity to gain mastery of skills.

Fine motor

For a student who has difficulty with written tasks, computers can allow him to produce written work using standard or alternative keyboards.

Play and recreation

Computers can provide an excellent recreation activity for students who are highly motivated by them. For students who find play time in schools a challenge, computer access can be an excellent play activity.

Independent work skills

Computer programs with a structured start and finish, and a set number of components to be completed, can be used to teach, promote and extend independent work.

Interaction

Computers can be used as a tool to teach the student to take turns and interact with his peers.

Motivation

The computer provides a non-threatening, predictable, non-intrusive, visual tool through which the student can more easily experience success.

Job opportunities

Computers can provide excellent future options for students, as they are suited to students' learning style and interest and require minimal social skills.

Important point to remember

As with any learning tool, computers need to be carefully monitored to ensure the student is successfully learning, by progressively moving on to new skills.

COMPUTER

Aims

- For the student to practise typing on the computer.
- For the student to use capitals, full stops, commas and the return key.
- For the student to locate letters on the keyboard.

Instructions

Many students have the same hesitations about typing on the computer as writing stories. By giving them the text they can focus on their typing skills.

Activity 1

Use the birthday cake worksheet. This requires the student to use capitals, full stops, commas, the return key and to locate a range of alphabetical keys.

Activity 2

Type word lists. You can use spelling lists or make up lists of words that interest the student. The days and months worksheet on p.63 could also be used.

Activity 3

Copy a reading book to make the student's own book of the same, or just practise typing. Use a favourite book or special interest and let the student type the text (see also the worksheet on p.90).

Activity 4

Type out daily schedules and timetables. You can make a master schedule and the student can fill in the activities.

Activity 5

Use COMPIC programmes, including the "Food for Thought" programme which is devised specifically for students with autism spectrum disorder. See www.edby design.com/ebdsw/index.html.

Activity 6

Visit web sites or even a chat room for people with autism spectrum disorder if the parents give you permission.

THE BIRTHDAY CAKE

This is a picture of a birthday cake.
There are four candles on the cake.

At a birthday party you sing, "Happy Birthday to you."
Then you blow out the candles.

Instructions

Type out the above sentences.
Print out your typing.
Draw a picture of a cake.
Colour the cake.
Draw someone blowing out the candles.

Extension activity

Type the words to the song "Happy Birthday."

TYPE ON THE COMPUTER

Aeroplanes fly in the sky.

Aeroplanes have wings and engines to help them fly.

A pilot flies an aeroplane.

Some planes take passengers.

Some planes take parcels or cargo.

Instructions

Type out the above sentences.

Bold the word "aeroplanes."

Italic all the words.

<u>Underline</u> the first word of each sentence.

Choose your font.

Print.

Draw a picture of a plane.

Type out the following sentences and fill in the missing words:

My name is _____

My address is_____

My birthday is _____

Today is _____

Tomorrow is _____

Yesterday was _____

The month is _____

The year is _____

The weather is _____

Chapter 8

Successful Strategies for Special Interests and Obsessions

The nature of autism spectrum disorder is such that students often have:

- an intense interest in one or two specific topics, often to the exclusion of all else, e.g. computers, jigsaws, transport, television shows, mechanical devices

- good motivation and achievement in a specific area of interest, while poor in other areas.

Special interests have the advantage of:

- increasing the student's motivation

- offering opportunities for success he may not achieve in other areas

- offering opportunities to teach further skills through using the special interest

- increased post-school options for work and leisure activities which involve his special interest

- offering opportunities for interaction with peers with similar interests.

Strategies

- Use the special interest as a motivation or reinforcement for completing other activities, e.g. "When you have completed these five activities you can draw trains for five minutes."

- Ensure you set limits (start and finish of special interest activities). Examples include the class finishing, the bell ringing, a timer ringing or beeping and using an egg timer or clock. It is extremely important that these limits are clearly understood by the student, otherwise you will not be able to move him onto less motivating activities.

- Use the special interest as an opportunity for interaction with peers. A student who is excellent on the computer could show other students how to use programs, or be the class "computer expert" for breakdowns. A student who is good at illustrating could give lessons to the class on how to draw. A student who loves names and routine could be in charge of role call each day.

- Broaden the focus of the special interest. If a student is only interested in one type of train, broaden his interests to more trains and transport to ensure he doesn't become too obsessive.

- Ensure the student has clear guidelines of when an activity starts and finishes, otherwise he may repeat the activity over and over and get so involved it is difficult to stop him. Verbally telling him he has finished is rarely heard when it is a special interest or obsession. Use a start and finish time; a schedule of the activity and a "finish" pictograph or pictograph of the next activity; or a clear end, e.g. the school bell.

SPECIAL INTERESTS

The following are ideas of the many different ways you can use a student's special interests. Some of these examples use transport as the special interest. However, you can replace transport with any other special interest.

Maths

- Counting activities.
- Matching activities.
- Shopping activities that include buying his special interest.
- Measuring activities that include measuring the size of different objects.

Fine motor skills

- Jigsaw: cut out a picture of his special interest and get him to cut and paste the pieces back together.
- Matching activities: make two copies of the transport pictures and get the student to cut and paste them.
- Drawing: get the student to draw his special interest.

Writing

- Let the student write or type about his interest when he has completed another writing activity.
- Use spelling activities that include one or two of his special interest words among other words.

Reading

- Make up his own reading books, which include his special interest.
- Use reading about his special interest as a reward, e.g. "Read five other books, then you can read *Thomas the Tank Engine.*"
- Make up comprehension activities which include his special interest, and questions about his special interest.

Social skills

- Board games, that include a special interest, can promote turn taking and waiting for a turn.
- Use computer games to promote social interactions (turn taking etc.).

Behaviour

- Use a special interest as a reward. Be careful not to overuse rewards!

SPECIAL INTEREST: TRANSPORT I

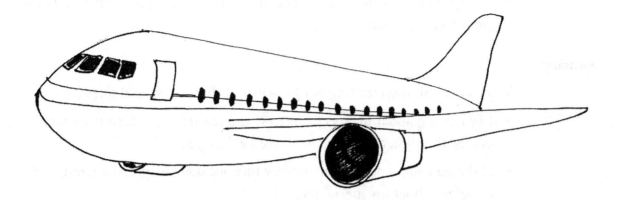

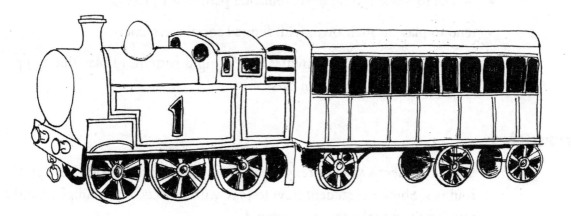

Chapter 9

Successful Strategies for Play

The nature of autism spectrum disorder is such that students often:

- have obsessive play routines (or special interest play)

- have a need for sameness

- do not follow a typical developmental pattern for playing

- tend to play on their own, with limited social interaction

- undertake unusual play activities and/or rigid patterns of play (lining up objects, spinning wheels on cars).

Strategies

- Use the student's visual strengths and rote memory to develop new play routines. Show the student how to play with objects. For example, build a train track and take the train around.

- Take photos of different ways to do activities; for example, building different types of towers using blocks.

- Teach the student turn taking through play. Board games are great for this. You can use photographs of students playing and put a marker on the picture showing whose turn it is and what colour she is using.

- Use schedules to develop play scripts. Photograph scripts are great. Take a photo of the different steps in an activity. See the examples of ideas for photoscripts in the following section.

- Many students love trains. They tend not to make the train tracks. To teach this, make a template for the student to put the tracks on. Use a large piece of cardboard and draw around the track, showing how the pieces connect.

- For turn taking with trains or cars, you can attach a small photo of the person whose turn it is to the top of the play activity.

Ideas for photo scripts for play

Take photos of all the steps. You might start with simple two-step activities and build up to ten steps.

Bathing baby:

1. Baby with clothes off.

2. Baby in the bath.

3. Baby having her nappy put on.

4. Baby being dressed.

Building a house with blocks:

1. Base plate.

2. Adding walls (can show each wall being added seperately).

3. Adding the door.

4. Adding the roof.

Doll's house:

1. Empty doll's house.

2. Show different furniture placement in different rooms.

3. Show different activities, e.g. family going to bed, family eating breakfast etc.

Playing trains:

1. Get the train set.

2. Get the cardboard.

3. Match the train tracks.

4. Put the train on the tracks.

5. Play trains.

Ideas for scripted play for students

Write out a script to help with play and language associated with play.

Let's build a tower

1. Ask a friend to play: "Will you come and play blocks with me?"

2. Get some blocks: "Let's build a big tower."

You can use a whole range of language depending on the students:

3. "Let's take turns. You go first."

4. "I will put on the blue blocks. What colour do you want?"

5. "Wow, it is getting big."

6. "Oh no, it fell down."

7. "Let's try to build another one."

Chapter 10

Successful Strategies for the Playground

The nature of autism spectrum disorder is such that students often:

- do not understand the rules of play

- find the vast open space of the playground confusing

- confine imaginative play to one or two themes

- are clumsy and uncoordinated at gross motor movements

- display a number of self-stimulatory motor movements (e.g. pacing, rocking)

- may be socially isolated but are not worried about it.

Strategies

Playtime is meant to be a stress release time for students, but for students with autism spectrum disorder playtime can be highly stressful and overwhelming. This may mean they return to class highly stressed and unable to participate.

- Allow the student to have time out by letting him be on his own or do activities he finds relaxing without constant adult supervision. See the following section on "School and classroom helper ideas."

- After playtime have a "time out" activity or relaxation area where the student can unwind if playtime was stressful. You could have a favourite worksheet, colouring activity, construction activity, special interest or personal stereo with relaxing music he can listen to, or roll him up in a gym mat and let him lie there for ten minutes. This could also be a physical activity such as running around an area of the playground before he comes inside if this is relaxing for him.

- Many students find a full hour too stressful at lunchtime. Make the playtime a manageable time for the student. This could include "time out" activities mentioned above or other activities listed below. Playtime could be split into 30 minutes' play and 30 minutes' other activities or 20 minutes' play, 20 minutes' other activities and 20 minutes' play.

- Use a schedule of activities the student can do in the playground (see "Schedules" on p.17).

- Use a business card wallet the student can keep in his pocket with ideas of activities he can do in the playground or conversation ideas.

- Set clear boundaries.

- Start a special interest club, e.g. chess club, computer club, mathematics club.

- Teach the student to ask if he can join in a game and how to react if other students say, "No." This will need to be taught in the control of the classroom at first and then the playground.

- See Chapter 4 on Social Skills for further details.

School and classroom helper ideas

If the activity is highly motivating you can use this as a reward. Many of the activities are great life skills for students for future jobs.

Library

- Reshelf books.

- Collect students' books which are being returned.

- Help students find books.

- Stamp due dates in books.

- Straighten books on shelves.

Art room

- Wash paint brushes.

- Put out paper for students.

- Sort pencils and colouring pens.

- Sharpen pencils.

Classroom

- Call roll (this is great for creating interaction).
- Collect and return students' work.
- Collect students' notes or money.
- Clean tables.
- Sort and sharpen pencils.

General school

- Water gardens and pot plants.
- Check physical education equipment is returned and tidy.
- Use school pencil sharpener (especially if you have an electric sharpener he likes).
- Take the video machine to classrooms who have booked it, rewind tapes etc.
- Check all lights have been turned off in classrooms before recess and lunch.
- Empty rubbish bins.
- Staff room – wash staff dishes, unload dishwasher, wipe down tables.

School office

- Photocopy something.
- Stamp envelopes.
- Count out notices and newsletters for classrooms.
- Deliver notes to classrooms.
- Notice boards and displays – remove old displays, put up new displays, ensure they are kept neat etc.

Computer

- If the student is a computer expert, get him to be the school computer technician.

Illustrations

- The student could be the school illustrator for newsletters, class or certificates and give lessons to other students.

Chapter 11

Successful Strategies for Sensory Issues

The nature of autism spectrum disorder is such that students are often hypo- or hyper-sensitive to sensory stimuli (over- or under-reaction to sensory information):

- Touch – by others and tactile materials.
- Auditory – certain noises.
- Visual – colours, visual distortion.
- Olfactory – certain smells.
- Taste – certain textures and flavours.

Strategies

- Ask an occupational therapist to devise a specific programme to access the student's needs.

- Teach the body parts and senses so the student can identify and tell you what is upsetting or annoying him. For example, if a student gets upset when a bus goes past, is it because of the sound, the colour of the bus, or the smell of the exhaust?

- Let the student use a personal stereo to listen to music for relaxation, cutting out noises etc.

- Let the student put his fingers in his ears if noises are annoying him.

- Create a quiet area, corner, desk or room he can go to if he is overwhelmed by noises.

- Use the sudent's favourite sensory activities for relaxation or reducing anxiety. Examples include rubbing the student's back during group instruction or high anxiety times, letting the student relax by chewing a soft mint (of course, you would monitor this carefully), letting a student who likes to feel a fabric have the fabric in his pocket to touch.

- If the student relaxes when swinging, take him to a playground with a swing.

- Read books about senses and encourage him to talk about different senses.

- Make a book about the student and his favourite tastes, smells, colours, sounds and items to touch.

- Get the student to do eye contact activities including flying a kite, throwing and catching, or throwing bean bags or balls at targets.

- Use shaving cream and finger paint.

- Use foot spa and washing activities.

- Cooking activities include all senses.

- Sensory activities

Sensory activities

Tasting and smelling game

Put a range of edible products in containers, so the student doesn't recognize the contents. Products with distinct taste and smell include toothpaste, vegemite, flour, sugar, coffee and vinegar. Let the student taste and smell them. Make this into a group game with other students for interaction and turn taking.

Visual activities

- Candles (these are also useful for their smell – there are a range of different scented candles on the market)

- Bubbles

- Blow up balloons of different colours

- Battery-operated toys that move

- Marble track game

Touch

(These activities also teach body parts.)

- Massage different body parts using cream and see the student's reactions to touch on his arms, legs, back, face and so on. Some may create laughter and some may create screams. Let the student massage other students so he touches other students also.

- Massage using an electric massager.

- Have different textures for the student to feel, including sand paper, brushes with a range of bristles, fabrics and hard and soft objects.

- Let the student feel a range of surfaces. Put sticky tape in loops, plastic wrap that pops, carpet, lino, silk or fur on the floor and let the student walk, crawl and run over the textures. These can also be used for feeling with his hands.

- Wrap different materials around the student's arms, legs, feet or head so he can feel different textures. Many students do not like changing their clothes – you may find this is due to textures. Some people with autism spectrum disorder can't stand the feel of labels in their clothes and insist they be cut out.

- Try applying deep pressure by wrapping up the student in sleeping bags, gym mats or blankets and then push or squeeze him. This can have a relaxing effect.

- Water or sand play activities.

- Fill a large container with rice, corn flakes or rice bubbles. Let the student do activities in the different textures – for example, play type activities: hide his favourite objects (e.g. Thomas the Tank Engine) in the rice and get him to find them.

Chapter 12

Successful Strategies for Programming and Specific Teaching Strategies

How to develop a successful programme

1. Research current information on autism spectrum disorder.

2. Profile the student (using the Profile of Individual Student form in this chapter).

3. Establish a Programme Support Group (PSG) to share information with parents, to set aims for the student and to define the roles of all the people involved with the student. (Use both the Individual Profile form and the list of target behaviours included in this chapter as guidelines for aims and objectives.)

4. Establish the support required to meet the objectives set by the PSG and IEP (Individual Education Plan).

5. Brief school staff on the student.

Successful teaching principles to enhance the student's learning

- Teach and maintain the ability to pay attention to people and tasks.

- Aim to extend the student's experiences and to teach him new skills.

- Teach the student how to use equipment appropriately, the meaning of a task and how to begin and complete it.

- Have high expectations and expect high quality performance at the targeted level.

- Teach the correct way first.

- Keep activities and language concrete, natural and meaningful for the student.

- Limit the use of prompts, and fade them as quickly as possible (e.g. a prompt could be pointing to the top of the page for the student to start).

- Avoid continuous one-to-one teaching – include group work daily.

- Work towards independence, keeping in mind the needs of the student as an adult.

Successful strategies to enhance performance in teaching situations

1. Obtain the student's attention.

2. Choose tasks which can be completed within the student's attention span.

3. Allow time for the student to think before expecting him to respond.

4. Maintain the student's attention, e.g. by saying "keep looking."

5. Don't comment on failure, just show the correct way.

6. Ensure that the task is relatively easy to complete.

7. Start the next activity straight away, once the student has successfully completed a task.

8. Present a variety of short activities in the same session.

9. Minimize distractions such as noise and movement within the room.

10. Initially present activities which the student finds relatively easy, particularity repetitive or sensory and motor tasks.

11. Use physical prompts, when necessary, to start an activity (e.g. holding the student's hand and physically guiding him to pick up the pen to start).

Strategies for staff supporting students in class

This is a useful guide for devising your own school handout, especially if you have a range of people working with students.

1. Don't overload the student with verbal directions. Keep directions or requests brief and concise.

2. Write tasks down, where needed.

3. Give the student time to comprehend requests, directions or discussions.

4. Give praise where due and encourage the student to participate within the class. (If you know the student has a correct answer or comment, encourage him to relay it, when appropriate, to the class.)

5. Take short cuts. Take the initiative and help the student by writing down the questions or topic headlines to help keep the student up to date.

6. Set the student up for success. Take the liberty of rewording exercises so that the student can easily comprehend what is expected.

7. Be in control! Have worksheets and activities that will "withdraw" the student and reduce behaviours. Withdraw the student if you think the behaviour is going to escalate.

8. Be precise and consistent in expectations or directions.

9. Ensure that the student has the appropriate texts and equipment prior to the commencement of each class. This will minimize confusion, time away from class and, above all, help the student concentrate on the job at hand.

10. Does the student need rules? If so, make sure that the student has them on hand or is familiar with them.

11. Follow the direction of the class teacher.

Target behaviours for successful classroom participation

If the student hasn't achieved the following behaviours, it is recommended to teach them. Where possible they should be your initial aims for the student.

Functional communication

- Asks for help when needed – this could be by verbal or non-verbal communication, e.g. signs or PECs (Picture Exchange Communications).

- Indicates choices.

- Protests in an acceptable manner.

Working independently on tasks

- Stays on tasks.

- Completes tasks in the allocated time.

- Follows a routine at the end of a work session (packs away).

Attending and participating in a group

- Sits appropriately.

- Does not interrupt.

- Looks at the teacher (or speaker).

- Participates and follows instructions.

- Participates in activities at appropriate times (waits for a turn).

Following class routines

- Follows classroom rules and routines independently.

- Locates his own possessions and returns to the appropriate place.

- Locates materials in the classroom as needed and packs them away when finished with them.

- Goes to various areas in the room or school when instructed.

- Makes the transition from one activity to the next when requested.

Appropriate classroom behaviour

- Works and plays without disrupting his peers.

- Waits for a turn appropriately.

- Occupies time between activities appropriately.

Following directions

- Follows simple instructions given to the group or to him directly.

- Follows two-step instructions.

Self care

- Addresses toileting needs independently.

- Undresses and dresses independently.

PROGRAMMING FOR STUDENTS WITH AUTISM SPECTRUM DISORDER

Instructions

Taking time to fill in the following forms will be most helpful for the staff working with the student. It is recommended the forms are completed at the end of the year or before any changeover of staff throughout the year.

Please copy the forms and have all relevant people complete one (teacher, teacher aide, specialist teacher, parents). Delete yes or no as appropriate.

PROFILE FOR INDIVIDUAL STUDENT

Student _____ Form completed by _____

Academic

Does the student have adequate fine motor skills?   Yes/No

What about pencil grips?   Yes/No

Will the student need a modified curriculum?   Yes/No
    If yes, in what?

What are the student's learning strengths?

What are the student's learning weaknesses?

Does the student pick up verbal cues (two- and three-step instructions)?   Yes/No

Does the student have independent working skills?   Yes/No

When is the student independent and successful?

When does the student need assistance?

Does the student complete work in the allocated time?   Yes/No

General comments:

Communication

Can the student ask for help?   Yes/No
    If yes, how?

Does the student raise his hand to seek adult assistance?   Yes/No

Can the student make choices?   Yes/No

How does the student communicate?

Can the student ask questions?   Yes/No

Can the student answer questions?   Yes/No

Can the student engage in conversations?   Yes/No

Can the student communicate his needs and desires?   Yes/No

Can the student recall experiences?   Yes/No

General comments:

Behavioural

Can the student stay on task?   Yes/No

Can the student use free time independently?   Yes/No

Can the student sit for extended periods of time?   Yes/No

How does the student tolerate classroom noise?

How does the student react to change and new experiences?

✓

How does the student express frustration?

Can the student calm himself down?   Yes/No
    If Yes, how?

Have you created a place for the student to have "time out" from the group?   Yes/No
    If yes, what was most effective?

How does the student cope in the playground?

What have been successful playground activities?

Has the student ever been aggressive toward other children or adults?   Yes/No
    If yes, why?

Does the student have disruptive behaviours?   Yes/No
    List any behaviours and successful strategies

General comments:

Social skills (including strategies that help the child to be successful)

How does the student respond to other children?

Can the student work closely with others? | Yes/No

Does the student share willingly? | Yes/No

Does the student make eye contact with adults and children? | Yes/No

Does the student wait quietly for a turn? | Yes/No

Does the student initiate conversation? | Yes/No

Does the student react appropriately to his emotions or others'? | Yes/No
    If not, how does he react?

Does the student have appropriate play skills? | Yes/No

How does the student participate at outside play times?

General comments:

General

What support has the student had in the past?

What do you recommend in the future?

What motivates the student (objects and activities)?

What are his special interests?

What are his dislikes?

Are there any sensory likes/dislikes (i.e. sounds, textures etc.)?

General comments:

What are the key priorities for school in term _____ year_____ ?

© Sue Larkey 2005

Chapter 13

Successful Strategies for Transition

The nature of autism spectrum disorder is such that transition can be extremely stressful. Changes big and small can trigger confusion, anxiety and problems. A new teacher, new classmates and a new classroom can be particularly stressful. If the student is keeping the same teacher or teacher aide this is just one less change; however, for some students it is the change of students or classroom that creates the confusion.

Typical changes in a new school year or term

Any of the following can create huge anxiety:

- changes in the timetable
- a different playground
- new school books or pencil case
- new classroom rules
- new arrangement of objects
- new teachers (e.g. specialist teachers)
- new school administration (e.g. principal).

Strategies

- Use visual timetables and visual cues to indicate changes.
- Send home the timetable as soon as possible. Then the parents can discuss the changes and the student can learn the timetable.
- Use photographs, for example, of new teachers, new students in the class or a new playground.

- Ensure the student has strategies to stay calm. These may include a quiet area, a personal stereo with calming music and a favourite book or activity.

- If the student has difficulty finding her way from one class to another, allocate "hall buddies," who help the student find the next class.

- Allocate a place where the student can go if she gets lost or to get help (e.g. front desk, school library, special education teacher's classroom). Choose a place that is easy to find and always has an adult to quickly help the student, before she becomes anxious. Ensure the staff in this area know the student and can help. It is a good idea for them to have a folder with the student's timetables, information and strategies – this ensures the student can be helped quickly. Practise with the student going to this area when she is calm.

- If the student has difficulty with organization, put strategies in place to help – have the required materials for each class in separate bags in her locker. (e.g. in her art bag include a smock, a pencil case, a map to find the classroom etc.).

- The playground can be a very frightening place. Allocate an area of the playground for the student to play in that will be within eyesight of teachers and has activities she will enjoy. Other strategies include getting her to use the library at lunch times or joining clubs.

- Ensure communication is established with parents (e.g. using a journal).

Useful Resources

Books

Attwood, T. (1998) *Asperger's Syndrome: A Guide for Parents and Professionals*. London: Jessica Kingsley Publishers.

Cumine, V., Leach, J. and Stevenson, G. (1998) *Asperger Syndrome: A Practical Guide for Teachers*. London: David Fulton Publishers.

Grandin, T. (1995) *Thinking in Pictures and Other Reports from My Life with Autism*. Sydney: Doubleday.

Gray, C. (2000) *The New Social Story Book: Illustrated Edition*. Arlington, TX: Future Horizons.

Janzen, J. (1996) *Understanding the Nature of Autism: A Practical Guide*. M.S. San Antonio, TX: Therapy Skill Builders.

Joosten, A. (2003) *Annette Joosten's Book of Cool Strategies: A Personal Social Script Workbook for Australian Primary-age Students*. Pilot edition. Brisbane: Book in Hand.

Larkey, S. and Durrant, H. (2004) *Together We Cook n Learn*. (Cookbook and teaching manual.) Niddrie, Victoria: Larmac Educational Resources.

Lawson, W. (1998) *Life Behind Glass: A Personal Account of Autism Spectrum Disorder*. Lismore, New South Wales: Southern Cross University Press.

Maurice, C. (ed) (1996) *Behavioural Intervention for Young Children with Autism: A Manual for Parents and Professionals*. Austin, TX: Pro-Ed.

Quill, K. (1995) *Teaching Children with Autism: Strategies to Enhance Communication and Socialization*. London: Delmar.

Sacks, O. (1993) *An Anthropologist on Mars*. Sydney: Picador.

Thomas, G. (1999) *Asperger Syndrome – Practical Strategies for the Classroom*. London: The National Autistic Society.

Websites of interest

To get you started, great websites with free downloads, samples, activities and autism spectrum specific information are:

- www.edbydesign.com/spec_ed.html – some fun games and activities
- www.TheGrayCenter.org – Carol Gray's site on social skills.
- www.larmac.com.au
- www.dotolearn.com
- www.icontalk.com
- www.autismtoday.com

For local autism information, contact your local Autism Association.

Pictographs and visual strategies sites

- www.compic.com
- www.setbc.org/res/equip/boardmaker/files.html
- www.mayer-johnson.com
- www.ovec.org/ride/Activities/Boardhints.htm
- www.nlconcepts.com/productsvb.htm

Professional services

Autism Consulting and Educational Services (ACES) conducts workshops for a range of parents, professionals and community groups to promote understanding and successful strategies for students with autism spectrum disorder.

- Workshops (two hour, three hour, or full day)
- Conference presentations
- Devising and supporting implementation of programmes
- Supporting students with autism spectrum disorder in mainstream schools.

For additional information, see www.suelarkey.com, phone (+61) 9420 8219 or (+61) 0417 835717, or email sue.larkey@optusnet.com.au. Any feedback would be most appreciated.

Index